CASH BUILDING STRATEGIES

HOW TO EARN REGULAR INCOME ONLINE

I0494348

ANTHONY EKANEM

ISBN 978-1-63997-274-6

Contents

Preface

We live in very uncertain times. The economic and financial environments of the world are anything but predictable. In some countries, production companies are folding up. In others, there is high unemployment and job losses. Many families are now living below the poverty line. Inflation and high cost of living is prevalent. No one is certain of anything anymore.

There is one thing we know is certain, however, and that is the fact that times are hard. People are doing all manners of things to make ends meet. However, just when they think they are making headway, life throws another curveball at them that strikes them out at the home plate.

Bills are piling up, the cost living is rising very high, and oil prices continue to fluctuate. You may have had a time in your life when working for a living seemed to be pushing you deep into a hole you cannot get out. If this is your experience, take a deep breath, relax and read this book to the end. There is light at the end of the dark tunnel for you. This book will help you turn your situation around by providing answers to the disturbing situation you find yourself.

You can earn a decent living online. You can rise and see the sunshine that others have seen. Take solace in the fact that inner peace is at your disposal, and we will show you how to find it by earning regular income online.

CHAPTER ONE

Breaking the Myths

Since we are talking about making money online, let us start by addressing the issue of internet fraud first. This is to clear all doubts and pave the way for you to decide the online business path you want to take.

Scam and *fraud* are so synonymous with the word *internet* these days. Many pessimists put down this way of making money just because the internet is involved. They will scream *scam* or *fraud* on the rooftops when they hear any kind of online money-making opportunity.

While there are scams and fraud in the online business space, there are also many legitimate opportunities to explore. Research will bring you a lot of information and tips to spot these scams, so you can move forward to earn a legitimate living from the comfort of your home.

Over the years, scams and frauds have grown in all areas of the internet. These have made people sceptical about doing any business online. There are so many legitimate ways to make money on the internet. Many people have successfully done so and continue to do so. Therefore, do not let this opportunity pass you because of doubts.

This book will show you how to make money legitimately online and how to avoid any nasty scammers that may want to prey on you or your loved one.

The more educated you are about internet scams and frauds, the more confident you will become when searching for an online business. Take control of your business future before someone else takes advantage of you. Let us bust some of the internet scam myths!

Here are some of the famous statements made by most of internet fraudsters and the truth behind them:

Myth 1: You Will Make Money Overnight!

This scam promises you a way of making money online while you sleep. They make it sound as if there is little or no work involved in doing it.

The Truth: While it is possible to achieve, it will take hard work and dedication to make money online. Most online businesses will take time to succeed but will be worth your effort in the end.

Myth 2: You Can Turn Your Computer into a Money-making machine! Many fraudulent statements start with this kind of sales pitch.

The Truth: The statement itself may be true but be very careful of any sales pitch that starts this way. Most legitimate online business opportunities sell the business itself. Scammers tend to sell the money-making benefit, and in that case, there is no business to do. To the scammer, they are making money off people paying them for what they say they will give them.

Myth 3: You Can Start your business Without money.

The scammers would push the fact that you can get a business going without money in start-up costs.

The Truth: This type of scam will scream the 'no money involved' statement but turn around to ask you to pay them for the information on how to get a business started for free. Are they not contradicting themselves? There are costs involved in starting a business, but very rarely do those costs break the bank.

Myth 4: You Can Start Earning a Living Typing at Home

This statement is like many others spread on the internet, claiming you can start a home-based business with your typing or data entry skills.

The Truth: Yes, you can earn money by typing or performing data entry from home, but not with people. You are better off offering these services to clients by yourself and avoid paying the fraudsters for the information on how it is done. You can always find out for yourself how to do it.

There are other internet scams. The ones mentioned above will give you an idea about how the frauds work and whom the fraudsters like to prey on. Know your options and don't be afraid to research any opportunity you don't feel comfortable with.

CHAPTER TWO

Getting Started

The fear of getting started tends to make many people procrastinate in starting their own business. That fear usually comes down to the fact that they don't know *how* or *where* to start. This chapter will take you through this process, so you can lay aside fears and move on to start your online business with ease.

Let us start by providing answers to some of the questions you may have.

1. ***Do you need any special skills or qualifications to start the business?***

You will need to have at least some basic knowledge in the field you are going into. It is not necessary to have any business or a university degree to start your own business. However, that will depend on the type of business you want to start.

A simple research in the field you want to go into will be enough to give you what you need in most cases. If you are planning to offer a service, like web designing, you should have some skills in that area before trying to start such a business.

University or college degrees and experience are always helpful in gaining expertise in a field. However, you don't need to have any degrees to have your own online business. Knowledge is very powerful online. So, reading everything you can lay your hands on that deals with your field is essential.

2. ***Will it cost you much money to start?***

Starting an online business does not generally cost much money. The money you will invest in it will be mostly for a computer system, internet access and a website. All other costs will be based on the type of business you want to do.

Businesses that you will sell items you have created will require some money to stock the items. However, you can find great deals on the internet for this purpose. If you plan to offer a service like web designing, you will need to add software programmes to your list of tools to buy.

For the most part, you will not have to run to your bank for a loan. Search for the best deals on the items you need for the business, and you will not have to worry about interest payment on a loan.

3. *Can you start the business even if you have not run a business before?*

Yes. Many Internet Marketers started their business and made a success of it without having any previous business experience. It depends on how much time and effort you put into your research.

The internet holds a plethora of information and can help you learn every aspect of the business you want to go into. You can find the tips, tricks and all sorts of information from people who have been there. So, utilise the internet to gain the power that knowledge will bring you.

4. *How much can you make from the online business?*

How much you can make depends on many factors. These include the type of business you go into, the amount of time and effort you put into it, and the return on investment on your business.

Some internet marketers make a six-figure income monthly, while others make the same amount a full-time fast-food worker typically makes. No matter how much your internet business brings in, you will still be ahead of those who commute to work. The money they spend on fuel, work clothes and meals is money that goes into your pocket and not someone else's.

5. *Do you need a website?*

You will need a website to conduct your business. In the course of your business, you will need to sell your products or show your potential clients the services you render. Your website will serve as your 'office' or 'storefront'. You will not need to rent an expensive space in a building to use for your online business.

Websites are simple to build if you use one of the various website design software or website building services. If you choose, you can also hire a web designer to create a professional website for your business. Do not allow the lack of web designing skills to hold you back.

6. *Do you need any licence to run an online business?*

You have to check with your local authorities what you will need in your area. Each area is different, so it is best to find out and see what you need before starting your business.

7. *How will you receive payments from your customers?*

If you are selling physical items, you may want to use an online payment system like PayPal. They will take care of the whole payment process for you, including refunds. Many times, shopping cart software will come with web-building software, so take advantage of that option.

CHAPTER THREE

Legitimate Online Businesses

There are several types of legitimate online businesses you can choose from. Listed below are the popular online businesses people get into and what each one entails. Check out each option to see which one suits your needs before you proceed.

1. **Service-Based Businesses**

A service-based business is one that offers some type of service to potential clients. Some of these include:

1. Writing
2. Web Design
3. Accounting/Bookkeeping
4. Virtual Assistant

Some small business owners have a hard time doing all their business tasks by themselves, so they outsource such jobs to someone else. They look for people that offer the services they require.

If you have experience in any of these areas, you could offer it as a service by starting your business in that line. For example, if you have some writing skills and experience and can write very well, you can offer that as a service to people who need contents for their websites.

Skills Needed

Depending on the type of service you want to offer your potential clients, you should have some skills under your belt. It is not necessary to have educational degrees to perform these services. However, clients like to see that you have the experience to complete the tasks they need to do.

Working online does not provide the face-to-face contact that brick and mortar businesses have when they hire employees. Trust comes a little harder online, so clients would like to know the person they are hiring has skills and knowledge in a specific field. It is not necessary to have many years of experience in a field. The fact that you have done a job before and have testimonials to back up your claim can help your business tremendously.

The Tools Needed

The working tools you need depend on the type of services you want to offer. The common ones that most service-based businesses should have include:

1. A Computer
2. Reliable Internet access
3. A Telephone
4. An Email
5. A Website

There will most likely be some software programmes to acquire as well. Each service uses different ones, but most would need a word and data processing application. You will also need a web designing programme – if web designing is among the services you will offer.

You should also consider having an Instant Messaging programme. Some clients would like to contact you instantly without having to use the telephone to call or wait for an email response.

How to Get Started

The first thing you should do is to decide on the type of service you are planning to offer your clients. Write down everything you can think of that shows you have experience or knowledge in a particular field.

Next, have your website created. Showcase your skills or experience on your website and provide prospective clients with testimonials from other people who have used your products or services and were pleased with the results. Place your rates and any additional information about how you run your business.

Market your website on various places on the internet to get your business out for potential clients to see. When clients contact you for whatever service they need, let them know how things will go. For instance, let your client know how they will pay for the job and how much it will cost.

It may take a while to build a list of regular clients, so do not expect to be making much money right from the state. Give your business time to grow and keep marketing it until it you acquire enough clientele.

Running a service-based business is the perfect option for those who are already doing that type of job. In some cases, you could make more money offering your services online than you can make by working a brick and mortar position.

2. Affiliate Marketing

Affiliate marketing is an online business where you sell other people's products or services and earn an income from the sale you made. Typically, you would earn a pre-determined amount (or percentage) of money based on the sales you make. However, in some cases, you could make money on the clicks from your website that get the consumers to the affiliate websites.

Sometimes, you can earn money by getting your site visitors to sign up for things on the affiliate websites, such as newsletters. Each affiliate programme will discuss this further on how they work, so when you sign up for their programme, be sure to check out how their processes work. They will keep track of your sales through an affiliate link that they provide you, which you place on your site.

What Skills Are Helpful

You don't have to be a professional salesman or a marketer to be an affiliate marketer. However, some knowledge of how to market or sell is essential. Learn everything you can about how online marketing works and how to be successful in affiliate marketing from top and successful affiliate marketers. It will take hard work and dedication to make your affiliate marketing business successful. If you don't have the time or the resourcefulness to work hard, don't do this as your online business.

What Tools Are Needed

The tools needed will be minimal. Besides the usual computer with reliable internet access, you will need a website to sell your affiliate products. You won't have to stock up on the products to sell them. Your website will need fresh contents regularly, so be prepared to either write some articles yourself or hire someone to do the writing for you. A blog to link to your website will be helpful as well to make the search engines happy with you.

How to Get Started

You will need to determine the niche for your affiliate marketing website. This will help you stand out from your competitors. For instance, you could use weight loss as your niche. Create your website based on the niche you have chosen for your business. After that, find affiliate products to sell from that website. Make sure the products you decide to sell relates in some way to the niche you have chosen for your affiliate marketing business. So, if your niche is in the weight loss field, you will want to offer affiliate products that relate in some way to weight loss. If you don't offer related products in your business, you run the risk of appearing as unprofessional and the search engines won't be happy with you either.

Many people make quite a lot of money running this type of business. It is important to remember that the most work you will have in this type of business will be marketing your website to get consumers to find you. When they find you, your website should be able to get them interested in your products to the point that they will buy using your affiliate links.

3. Selling on E-Bay

This is another popular online business that many people are doing. E-Bay is a very popular online auction website that millions of people use every day to find deals on items they want to buy.

You can sell anything you have at home that you no longer need as well as items using the drop-ship method. If you search the e-Bay website, you will see a variety of items that people are selling. These could be either used items or brand new ones that come from wholesalers. In either case, people will pay good money if you provide them with what they are looking for. Some people go so far as buying items from open markets and garage sales for the sole purpose of reselling them on e-Bay for a profit.

What Skills Are Helpful

You don't need any special skills to sell items on e-Bay. The ability to market and promote your items on the eBay site will be the most important one to have. People can search the website for the things you are selling. However, if you want to make money in this line of business, you have to market those items elsewhere to get people to find them. If you are selling items from home, take a good photo of the items so people can see them.

What Tools Are Needed

The only tool you would need to start this type of business is an account with e-Bay to sell your items. If you plan to use the drop-ship method, you will have to find wholesalers that will ship the items direct to the customers. Access to a computer with reliable internet access will be necessary to keep track of your sales. You will also need a payment processor account like PayPal to receive money from your customers.

How to Get Started

To start, you have to sign up for an account with E-Bay that allows you to sell from there. Try to buy items from the site as well to help build your user ratings, so people will have confidence in buying from you. Place photos, if possible, of the items you want to sell. Items that have a picture sell much faster than those that do not have. People like to see what they are buying; so, provide them with the best quality photo possible.

Review all informational materials and the rules on the eBay website, to get tips on how to make more sales and how the process of selling on the E-Bay site works. Selling on eBay is a good way to start your online business. This gives you your first taste of an online business without having to stock much equipment to get started. Also, you have the benefit of getting rid of undesired items in your home while you make a little money on the side.

4. Making Money from Membership Sites

Some online business owners make money from selling memberships on their websites. People buy memberships to gain access to contents that the website owner provides them regularly.

For example, you may offer memberships to internet users who need articles for their websites. Membership would need to be renewed every few months or so, depending on how long your membership is valid. Each time someone renews their membership, you make money.

The profit potential for this kind of business is high. It will not cost much to provide your members with informational products. However, you can charge them a decent amount to access them, giving you a profit that keeps on giving.

What Skills Are Helpful

Marketing skills will be the most helpful. Getting internet users to visit your site to buy your memberships is what will make you the money. Having some knowledge of how to run a website could be useful to keep your website running smoothly for your members. You may also want to have some understanding of the products you are offering. For instance, if you are offering articles to your members, you should know what makes an excellent article and how they work for different purposes.

The Tools You Will Need

You will need a high-quality and well-designed website to handle the demands that a membership site brings. You should provide excellent services should anything goes wrong with the website. There is inexpensive membership site management software that can help you get set up and running within a short time.

Contents for your website is another tool you will need. You need to provide your paying members with fresh materials to use regularly. It could be in the form of written articles, software programmes or even online games, depending on what you plan to give your members.

How to Get Started

You will need to plan your membership website. What do you want to offer your members? Will it be contents or software? Once you have decided on what to offer your members, you can then come up with ways to provide service to them. You could offer contents in a specific niche, like nutrition, or you could provide a broader kind of written materials. Whatever it takes, provide your members with fresh contents regularly to enjoy. This helps you stand out from the crowd of competitors out there.

Next, get a shopping cart feature added to your membership website to handle the payments from your members and user. The membership management software should come with all you need to succeed in your business. All you would then need is the contents to give to your members. The most critical step, after that, will be to market your membership site to get people to find you. Marketing techniques will be discussed later.

Membership sites can offer you a means to earn residual income. If people are satisfied with what you offer them, they will have no problem paying you to keep renewing their access to your website's contents.

5. Making Money From Selling Products

You can do this type of business in different ways. One way will be to create and sell your products. Crafters or creators often get into this form of business to sell their crafts and creations. Most creators of scrapbooks choose this path for their business.

Another way to sell your products is to use an online store that sells different products. There would be no items to stock in your home, nor do you have to ship anything directly from your location. The products will be ordered through the 'store' you have set up and the wholesaler providing the products will ship the items directly to the customers on your behalf.

Helpful Skills

The skills you need here are the ability to work hard and excellent customer service. You will spend much time marketing your websites so that potential customers will find you. Having a good website is necessary to provide your customers with everything they need when deciding whether to buy your products.

Customers may have questions about the products and may also have issues that you will need to address; therefore, excellent customer service skill is a must. Establishing a rapport with your customer will bring repeat patronage and referrals. Provide them with top-notch customer service, and this will help you gain credibility.

What Tools Are Needed

If you have chosen to sell the products that you create yourself, you will need to stock up your inventory. Check with vendors to find good deals on things that are bought in bulk to help you save money. Of course, a website will be needed as well, as your customers will need to find your products to buy them. Make sure the site has a shopping cart feature to make the purchasing process seamless.

How to Get Started

The first thing you should do is to decide what you are going to sell. Are you creating your own products to sell, or are you planning to sell other products using drop shippers? If you are planning to sell any items you created yourself, you will need to research vendors for the materials you will need to make the products. Have some produced ahead of time, so that when consumers start to place orders, you can ship them out immediately?

When you are done with the planning stage, you will need to get your website created to sell your products. Make sure the website is easy to navigate, and it is not distracting that visitors get turned off from your business within a few moments. The last step in getting started in this business is to market your products. This step is the most important if you want your business to succeed, so don't hold back on it.

Selling products is an excellent way to make money online. If you have created a product to give away as gifts to friends and family, there is no reason you should not take the product to the internet and start selling them.

If you like the idea of selling products, but don't want to create one yourself, you can still do this kind of business by having someone else ship the products for you. Getting started this way gives you the flexibility to spend the time needed with your family while earning a living online.

6. Making Money with PLR Products

Private Label Rights (or PLR) product, is written content that can be sold to others to use for whatever purpose they want to use it. Website owners use these to get materials for their websites. It does not sound like a money-making opportunity when described that way. The truth is, the same package of written contents can be sold several times to other people. Here is how it works.

For instance, let us assume you are selling a package of 10 articles - all about a topic, like weight loss. Typically, these packages are sold for $1 each. Someone who has a website about weight loss needs articles to place on their site, so they buy a package from you. You just made $10. Now, that same package of 10 articles can be sold over and again. In the end, you can sell the ten articles 50 times, bringing you a total of $500 just for that one package. You can sell more than one set of PLR products at the same time, thereby increasing your profit potential.

Everyone charges a different amount and offers different types of PLR products. You can sell eBooks as well as articles. People can take these articles, change them to their needs and use them however they want.

Some Helpful Skills

Writing skills would be necessary. You would need to write good quality articles even though the people that buy them may modify them. You could hire a ghostwriter to write them for you, but keep in mind; you would have to pay them for their time, so this is a good option if you do not mind sharing your profit. Marketing your PLR contents would also be necessary. To make money in this business, you will need to get people to find your contents, so pull out all the stops when starting this business.

The Tools You Will Need

If you are going to write the articles yourself, you would need a computer with word processing software installed. A website will also be required to sell your PLR products. If you choose to hire a ghostwriter to write the contents for you, then you will need to find someone that fits your budget and provides good quality contents.

How to Get Started

Where to start is to get the articles written. Make sure that the package of articles that you will sell together relate to a topic. Topics could include gardening, pet care, nutrition, weight loss or exercise.

Decide how much you will sell the articles and get a website set up to sell them. You can use a website that provides the service of selling them for you, but you could be better off selling them on your website.

There is money in selling PLR products as there are millions of websites that need contents for their survival. With proper marketing techniques, you can earn a living from Private Label Rights business.

7. Make Money Selling Information Products

The internet is a great place to sell knowledge. Many people will pay any amount to get the information they desperately need. If you have the information product that people need, you could earn a substantial income from it.

Information products come in various forms, including:

1. E-Books
2. E-Courses
3. Tutorials
4. Guides
5. Podcasts
6. Audiobooks

These are popular information products that are sought after by internet users around the world. If you have something to say or a story to tell, this could be the business for you.

What Skills Are Helpful

You should have a good knowledge of the topic you are going to present to your customers. It is not necessary to have a doctorate of any kind to do this type of business, but having good knowledge in the subject matter would be helpful. The ability to market your products is also essential. The more people you reach with your products, the more people that may want to buy from you.

What Tools Will Be Needed

The tools you will need depends on what you plan to sell. E-Books and How-to Guides could be written using word processing software and then converted to a PDF, which is the most popular type of document people want.

You will need an autoresponder to create successful e-Courses. Podcasts would require audio recording and editing software. You could use a PowerPoint to present your materials, or you could use video tutorial software. Video tutorials are great for showing users how to use a specific programme step by step. You will also require a website or blog to promote your information products.

How to Get Started

You will need to decide on a topic for your information product. What do you have very good knowledge about that you can offer your potential customers? When you know what you want to offer, then research that topic to see if you can find a new and unique angle to present it in.

Since there are lots of E-Books and tutorials on the internet for sale, you will need to find something new to give to your customers. They may not be willing to spend their money if they think you don't have something unique to offer them.

Write or record your information product and edit it to your satisfaction. Once you have it the way you want it, you can start selling it. Create a blog or website to sell it and make sure the website's copy content grabs the internet user's attention so they can buy what you are selling.

You may have to hire a copywriter to write the sales copy for you if you can afford one. They can write contents in a way that makes your product so desirable that anyone would want to buy it.

Creating information products does not cost much, but you can sell them for a decent profit. This is an excellent way to earn income online while maintaining a flexible schedule that allows you to spend more time with your family.

8. Make Money Blogging

Blogging started many years ago as a way for people to connect with others and share their stories and experiences. It was considered a great personal journal that one could use to leave their mark on the internet. Blogs later evolved to become excellent marketing tools as well as a medium to make money.

There are various ways you can make money from blogging. Here are some of them:

1. **Ads Placement**. Search engines like Google and Yahoo offer a way to earn money with any blog or website. The idea is to place these advertisements on your site, and when a visitor clicks on them, you earn a pre-determined amount of money. The more clicks you get from your website visitors, the more money you will make. There are policies that govern these programmes, so if you choose to go this route, you must learn the do's and don'ts before you sign up for the programme.

2. **Product Reviews**. There are websites you can sign up with that can connect you with companies that need people like you to review their products and get them exposure on your blogs. Usually, the main requirement is a blog that has been around for a while and has a good number of visitors. The companies would pay you some amount of money to review their products on your website or blog.

3. **Contextual Links**. Some business or website owners will pay you to post their links on your blog posts. It could be the business owners themselves contacting you or a company that acts as their agent. Those businesses will find blogs and websites that relate to their company's product offerings, so the links provided on the blogs should be search engine-friendly. This is a great way to earn extra traffic for your website.

4. **Sell products**. Blogs are another place you can sell your products or the products of others for a commission. Those who have businesses selling home decoration or food items use blogs a lot to sell their products online.

Skills Needed

There is no much skill needed except the ability to write good and fresh contents, and the ability to market your blog. You may want to research blogging as much as possible to learn the tricks of the trade.

Tools Needed

Your main tool, apart from a computer with an internet connection, would be a blog. There are many blogging platforms to choose from, including WordPress and Blogger. Some are free to set up, while others require a monthly or annual fee to get started. The paid version of most blogging platforms can help you connect with other blogs and increase traffic to your site. The free versions are quite easy to set up, and some are very popular with bloggers. Therefore, finding people to connect with would not be a problem.

How to Get Started

Sign up with a blogging platform and start posting contents. Make sure you post regularly, at least two times a week. Blogs that are not updated periodically tend to get lost in cyberspace.

Market your blog as much as possible. Get listed on blog directories. Visit other blogs and comment on them to get some links back to your blog. The more traffic you drive to your blog, the higher your chances of making good money from your blog.

Most of the blogging platforms have a sign up for AdSense Ads already included in their set up feature, so getting started with AdSense will be easy. And if you want to provide product reviews and contextual links, you have to blog for a while and have a good amount of traffic coming to your

Blogging is an easy way to earn extra income if you work hard at marketing it. Those who are successful at blogging for money use every route to make their blog known in the internet community—those who don't earn little or nothing.

Become a successful blogger and make money off your blog. Don't blog as a hobby by posting once in a while. Make it a business and post contents as frequently as possible. Your bank account will thank you for it.

9. Making Money Coaching Others

A coach is someone who shares their knowledge in a particular field with other people who want to be successful in that field as well. Coaches can be experts in any field, from writing to blogging, and other areas of human endeavour.

If you have good knowledge or experience in a particular area, you can become a coach and make money doing it. Many coaches help others in web design, graphic design and even in the coaching field as well. A coach would offer guidance and techniques to people within that field, and answer questions throughout their coaching period and beyond.

What Skills Are Helpful

The most important skill you need to have for this type of business is the ability to listen and communicate well with others. You should also have great patience with your clients. Those who hire you to coach them want you to listen to their experiences and guide them.

To build rapport and credibility in this business, you must know your field well. If you have never designed a website before, you cannot be a web designing coach. This is because your lack of experience will be spotted right immediately, and trust will be lost.

The Tools You Will Need

You should have the following tools to do this kind of business:

- A Computer System
- An Email programme
- A Website
- Contents for your website
- Payment processor on your website
- Dedicated telephone line

Most of your conversations with clients will probably be through email. However, some people will be more comfortable talking to you directly.

How to Get Started

Plan your business. What services will you be offering? Get some articles, and other written contents created and place them on your website to build credibility and expert status for your business.

Explain on your website how your services work. Include testimonials from people who had used your services before and were pleased with the results. Make your website easy to navigate, so visitors don't get lost trying to find information about your coaching business.

Market your coaching business to attract clients. Plan the goals that the client wants to achieve by employing you, and discuss how those goals will be achieved. Listen to their concerns and questions and provide insightful answers and support to keep them moving forward to their goals.

Coaches who have good knowledge or experience in a specific area are well sought after. Use what you know about a topic and provide a coaching service to others to help them become expert in the same field.

10. **Make Money Researching**

This is a good business opportunity for those who like to learn and research about our ancestors. Genealogists make a living by creating family trees for people who do not have the time or patience to do it themselves.

Almost everyone likes to know their history and what their ancestors did that to contribute to the world. You can cash in on their curiosity by doing the research for them and providing them with their family heritage.

What Skills Would Be Helpful

Excellent research and organisational skills will be needed. These skills are what genealogy is all about. You will need to know how and where to carry out your research on each family's heritage and be able to put all the information in an easy to understand format for your clients.

What Tools You Would Need

You would need a computer with a reliable internet connection. You would have to subscribe to some of the best genealogy websites available to use for your research. You will also need to invest in some guides or attend classes to learn the tips and tricks on researching family trees.

A website would be needed to run your business. Clients will need to know how you perform your work and how much you charge. Provide some samples if possible, to show clients how thorough your job is.

How to get started

Bring all your supplies together and find genealogy websites to subscribe. Create a website to sell your service and start marketing your business to get clients. Utilise your internet resources as well as local libraries, courthouses and historical societies for your research. You may need to interview a few people to gather some information.

Create a family tree document that will hold all the family heritage information or use software programmes that provide that for you. If you love to research and are interested in historical records, you should be considering this type of business. Meet the demands that people have to find out their family history and make money doing something you love.

11. Make Money with Desktop Publishing

If you are creative and can use a computer well, consider an online business with desktop publishing. It is where you create documents, flyers, brochures, calendars, and advertisements. All these types of documents are created using one programme or the other from your computer, so you don't need any expensive equipment to create them. Many people are looking for these creative documents for all kinds of uses. If you have good knowledge in this area, you can use it to make money.

What Skills Are Helpful

The ability to use some word processing and desktop publishing software is required. You don't have to be a graphic artist to do this business as everything is done using the computer.

What Tools Are Needed

Besides a computer system, you also need to have the following:

- Desktop publishing software
- Photo editing software
- Laser or Color Printer
- A Scanner
- High-Quality printer paper

Make sure you know how to use all the features of the relevant computer application well so you can provide the best quality service for your clients.

How to Get Started

Acquire all the necessary tools to run your business. Decide on a niche to target your marketing efforts and create a website to reflect that niche. Your website should provide potential clients with samples of your work to show your expertise in the field. You may need to brush up your skills by reading tutorials or guides on desktop publishing.

Desktop Publishing can be a lucrative business for anyone who loves creativity. So, if you are creative and can use relevant computer software, then a desktop publishing business is for you.

12. **Creating A Business from Uncommon Ideas**

We have discussed the conventional means of starting an online business. There are some unconventional means as well that you can consider. By unconventional means, I mean those ideas that people came up with but were mocked by others. Those people then took those ideas and made a considerable living from them. Here are a few of those ideas that people thought would not get off the ground:

1. **Selling old seminars**. One young man made a decent living by finding and selling old seminars.

2. **Domain names**. Someone came up with the idea that they could sell a service of naming domains for other people. Sounds crazy, but the business took off. It turned out that quite a few people needed that service.

3. **Selling used engagement jewellery**. This idea reportedly came from someone who broke off their engagement, got the ring back but found they could not return it for full value. They created a website for other people in the same situation to sell their jewellery and earn back what they paid for it or as close to it as possible.

CHAPTER FOUR

Marketing Your Online Business

Now that you have known the different types of online businesses to choose from, the next thing is to learn how to market your business to make it successful. Let us explore some of the popular strategies for marketing an online business.

1. WEBSITE

Your online business website is the best place to start the discussion. If there is one thing that could make or break your business, it would be the website itself. Here are some things that are important to know about your website for marketing purposes:

a. **Domain name.**The domain name is the address to find your site on the internet. Choose a domain name that matches your website or business name. This helps internet users to find your business quickly if they are searching for a topic. An exact match would be the best option, but if it is not available, try finding one that comes as close to it as possible.

b. **Your Keywords.**Utilise the best keywords within the contents on your site. Keywords are words that internet users use when they go online to find information on a specific topic. The keywords would get indexed by the search engines and placed within the results page for a user. The higher your website is ranked on the results page, the more chance that the user will choose your website to visit.

c. **Market with a Niche**. A niche narrows down your business to a specific group of people. You are narrowing down your marketing efforts to a smaller group to help you give what your consumers want. Larger groups have too many people with too many different needs. This makes it challenging to get your audience interested in what you have. The smaller groups will be the people that are more likely to want what you have, so marketing will be much easier.

Your website should reflect the niche you have chosen for your business. If you are targeting mothers with young children, your website should reflect that. You would have graphics that would connect to mothers with young children, and the contents on the website should be written to something they can relate to. This will help with the search engines as well.

d. **Blog**. You may need to create a blog to go with your website. It should relate to the theme your business website has. Personal blogs should not be used here. If you are using a blogging platform that is not connected to your website, design your blog's template to match the theme of your business website.

Blogs are another way to utilise search engines to gain visitors. When a visitor lands on your blog, they would see that you have enough contents for them on the relevant topic.

2. EMAIL MARKETING

Emails are essential to any marketing campaign. This is how you keep your business fresh in your customer's and website visitors' minds. Getting visitors to your website is one thing. Getting them to remember your w over the millions of other websites is another thing; especially when they are interested in buying.

Emails come at regular intervals to provide information to website visitors to help build credibility as well as get your business name registered in their minds. You can do this in different ways. To get email addresses to send your messages to, you will provide an email opt-in form on your website. Your visitors can sign up for updates on what you are offering or for more information.

3. NEWSLETTERS

These are used to provide small articles on topics that relate to your business. For example, if you sell vitamins and minerals, your newsletter can offer articles on alternative health practices to show how important your product is to them.

You would regularly send Newsletters to their email with a link to your website for the full article. This enables users to become familiar with your website and makes it easier to remember you when they want to buy something you are offering.

4. E-COURSES

You can have a signup feature on your website for visitors to use to learn the basics about a topic. If you are selling vitamin products, you can use an e-course to teach your readers how to pick the best ones for different kinds of health issues. E-courses are typically sent over a 5 to 7-day period and are often offered for free. This keeps your business name in their minds by reminding them every day the e-course comes into their inbox.

5. UPDATES

For your customers or subscriber, you can provide them with updates on your products and services as well as discounts and freebies. This way, if you cannot hook a visitor into buying from you on their first visit, they may see something on their subsequent visits that catches their attention and entices them to buy. The updates can also help bring in more traffic for your website. Those who have already signed up for your mailing lists will have friends, family, neighbours and co-workers that they could refer to your business by forwarding the messages.

6. ARTICLES AND OTHER CONTENTS

Besides providing good website contents, articles and other contents can be used in several ways to market your business. Here are some of those ways:

A. **Article Directories**: Article Directories provide excellent marketing opportunities for your business. By writing and submitting an article related to your business, you can achieve two things:

i. Credibility in the topic you have written about
ii. Drive more traffic to your website by providing a link to your business website in the author's bio section provided on the article directory site.

These directories typically rank well with search engines. So someone stumbling on one of your articles in a directory can find their way to your website for more information on that topic.

B. **Guest Blogging**: By being a guest writer on someone else's blog or newsletter, you can reach more people looking for information on a topic. You would provide a link back to your website within the articles. You can then reciprocate the favour for the other website owner to provide the same kind of articles on your newsletters or blogs.

C. **Articles on *Digg* or similar websites:**Submitting one of your articles on *Digg* or other similar websites will drive traffic to your website. *Digg* is a website that provides articles that internet users deem useful and informative. The articles that receive many "Diggs" will be published on their home page where many users will see and review them. You can include your website link for those people who want more information on the topic.

D. **Offer E-books or Guides**: These can provide your website visitors with information on a topic while including a link back to your website to keep them familiar with your business. These can be offered for free or for a small fee. You would provide some necessary information on a topic. You could get them interested in buying an e-Book that has more in-depth information about the same issue.

7. SOCIAL MARKETING

One of the most successful ways to find targeted traffic is to socialise with like-minded people. Here are the most popular ways to socialise for your marketing needs:

a. **Blog Comment**ing. Find other blogs that are in the same niche as yours. Post a reply on some of their posts. Your website link will be associated with your name, and those looking for more information on that topic will visit your website or blog.

b. **Join Forum Communities**: Find message boards that have topics that relate to your website. Your website link could go in the signature line, allowing others to find their way to the website to see what you have.

Check with the rules of the board first to make sure this is permitted. By posting regularly on these forums, you can build credibility as an expert for that topic and gain some trust with some potential consumers who may be thinking about buying from you. Also, the other board members may refer people they know to your website, so make sure you give back as much as you receive with these communities.

c. **Social Media Sites**: Social media include popular Facebook and MySpace. These sites attract people of similar interests. Internet marketers use them all the time to hook up their target audience. People who have the same interest as you can communicate and start building trust. They will be more prepared to buy from someone who is in their "group", or they could pass your business information to other people they know.

1. **MISCELLANEOUS TECHNIQUES**

Here are some other techniques to use in your marketing campaigns:

i. **Affiliate Programme**: Start an affiliate programme for your products. Your affiliate will make money on each of the products they sell. More traffic will find its way to your site through other people's efforts. Learn how to start your successful affiliate programme and create a webpage on your website for others to sign up as affiliates. It is something that you can announce in your newsletters and update messages.

ii. **Google Adwords**: Search engines offer this feature to business owners to buy advertising space on search results pages. Every time someone clicks on the advert, you will be charged a certain amount of money by the search engine. Because you are paying for the clicks, you will need to provide the most desirable advert possible to increase your return on investment. A poor advertising campaign can cost you money because not everyone who clicks through your ads will buy. Keep track of these ads and pull them or revamp them when necessary to avoid losing money.

iii. **Word of Mouth campaign**. This is the most straightforward marketing technique available. A simple word of mouth will get people to pass on the information of your business to other people. It works well for local customers and clients. It is also a less expensive way to market your business.

iv. **Use Press Releases.** You can use this option if you are offering a discount or exclusive sale. Press Releases are submitted to websites that publish them for internet users who are looking for specific information. Press releases are written as if they are news stories and showcase your "news" with eye-catching and attention-grabbing headlines and information. Your sale, discount or business start-up would get plenty of exposure to potential customers and clients.

A well-written press release to announce what you are offering may be what you need to drive a considerable amount of traffic to your business website. Consider having one done periodically to help keep your business' name fresh on people's minds.

v. **Podcasting.** A podcast is audio content that creators use to provide information that people listen to instead of reading the written version. Podcast gives people a different medium to learn about a topic they are interested in. People love to listen to podcasts while they are doing something else. Your business gains credibility and trust amongst your listeners. Those listeners can become customers, so your website will be linked to the audio programme.

Epilogue

You can start and run your online business, whether you have business experience or not. All you need is the passion for success, and the ability to work hard and learn as much as you can about the business you are going into.

With the numerous options available for online business, you can find one that meets your needs and your skills. Use as many marketing methods as you can to get your business across to all corners of the internet world and drive traffic to your website. The hard work you put into it at the initial stage will pay off as you can take a break or hire someone else to perform some of your daily tasks for you.

The internet brings more and more money-making opportunities to business owners every day. So, get on the bandwagon and start reaping the rewards other internet marketers are reaping. If they can do it with little experience in the business field, so can you.

Good luck!